W9-BUV-293

BACH 02/14

LONG BEACH PUBLIC LIBRARY
101 PACIFIC AVE.
LONG BEACH, CA 90822

TEAM SPIRIT ®

SMART BOOKS FOR YOUNG FANS

THE DENVER BRONCOS

BY
MARK STEWART

NORWOOD HOUSE 🏠 PRESS

CHICAGO, ILLINOIS

Norwood House Press
P.O. Box 316598
Chicago, Illinois 60631

For information regarding Norwood House Press, please visit our website at:
www.norwoodhousepress.com or call 866-565-2900.

Editor: Mike Kennedy
Designer: Ron Jaffe
Project Management: Black Book Partners, LLC.
Special thanks to Topps, Inc.

Library of Congress Cataloging-in-Publication Data

Stewart, Mark, 1960-
    The Denver Broncos / by Mark Stewart. -- Rev. ed.
        p. cm.
    Includes bibliographical references and index.
    Summary: "A revised Team Spirit Football edition featuring the Denver
Broncos that chronicles the history and accomplishments of the team.
Includes access to the Team Spirit website which provides additional
information and photos"--Provided by publisher.
    ISBN 978-1-59953-521-0 (library edition : alk. paper) -- ISBN
978-1-60357-463-1 (ebook)
    1. Denver Broncos (Football team)--History--Juvenile literature. I.
Title.
    GV956.D37S74 2012
    796.332'640978883--dc23
                                                2012015466

Manufactured in the United States of America in North Mankato, Minnesota.
205N—082012

COVER PHOTO: The Broncos celebrate a good play during the 2010 season.

33090022569158

Table of Contents

CHAPTER	PAGE
Meet the Broncos	4
Glory Days	6
Home Turf	12
Dressed for Success	14
We Won!	16
Go-To Guys	20
Calling the Shots	24
One Great Day	26
Legend Has It	28
It Really Happened	30
Team Spirit	32
Timeline	34
Fun Facts	36
Talking Football	38
Great Debates	40
For the Record	42
Pinpoints	44
Glossary	46
Overtime	47
Index	48

ABOUT OUR GLOSSARY

In this book, there may be several words that you are reading for the first time. Some are sports words, some are new vocabulary words, and some are familiar words that are used in an unusual way. All of these words are defined on page 46. Throughout the book, sports words appear in **bold type**. Regular vocabulary words appear in *bold italic type*.

Meet the Broncos

The Denver Broncos know all about patience. They played 17 seasons before making it to the **playoffs** for the first time. Denver fans then had to wait another two *decades* before the Broncos won their first championship. It felt so good that the team went out and captured another title a season later!

Broncos fans demand the best from their team. That doesn't mean that they expect Denver to win the **Super Bowl** every year, but they always want to see a championship effort. That is what makes the Broncos a fun team to watch. They play exciting football.

This book tells the story of the Broncos. Through more than 50 years of ups and downs, two things have never changed. First, the Broncos find amazing players who can score at any time, on any play, from anywhere on the field. And second, Denver fans never stop believing that their team is ready to have another super season.

Von Miller and Ryan McBean celebrate a Denver victory. This kind of team spirit makes the Broncos fun to watch.

Glory Days

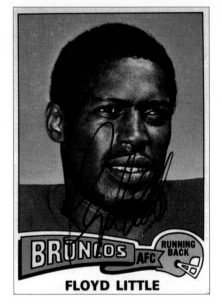

FLOYD LITTLE

Before traveling by jet became possible in the 1950s, Denver, Colorado, was considered too far away from other big cities in the United States to host a major sports team. Things began to change in 1960. That year, the **American Football League (AFL)** played its first season, and the Broncos took the field as one of the league's eight teams.

Over the next decade, the popularity of *professional* football *skyrocketed*. That helped the AFL attract lots of new fans. Eventually, the older **National Football League (NFL)** decided to merge with the AFL and form one league. Denver fans were happy that the Broncos were part of a big success story.

Denver had many good players in the team's early years, including Lionel Taylor, Eldon Danenhauer, Gene Mingo, Frank Tripucka, Floyd Little, Bud McFadin, Al Denson, and Rich Jackson. But it was not until the 1970s that the Broncos began winning on a **consistent** basis. Coach John Ralston helped turn the team around after he became the coach. Ralston built a strong defense called the "Orange Crush." Its leaders were Tom Jackson, Louis Wright, Lyle Alzado, and Randy Gradishar. The team's offense featured fast and exciting players, including Haven Moses,

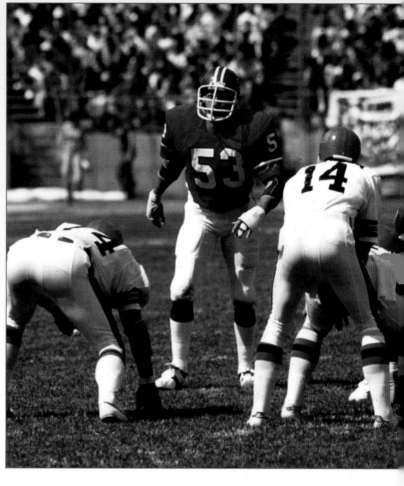

Riley Odoms, Otis Armstrong, and Rick Upchurch.

Red Miller took over for Ralston in 1977, and Denver fans sensed that something special could happen. That season, Miller made Craig Morton the starting quarterback and turned the defense loose on opponents. The Broncos went 12–2 and reached the Super Bowl for the first time. They lost to the Dallas Cowboys.

LEFT: Floyd Little signed this trading card. He was the team's best player in the 1960s.   **ABOVE**: Linebacker Randy Gradishar faces the Cincinnati Bengals during the 1970s.

Now that the Broncos and their fans had a taste of winning, they were hungry for more. In 1981, Dan Reeves was hired as the Denver coach. Two years later, the Broncos **drafted** strong-armed quarterback John Elway. He was an amazing athlete who had a knack for making big plays. No lead was ever safe with Elway on the field.

Reeves and Elway guided the Broncos to the Super Bowl three times, but Denver came up short of its first championship. The team's luck finally changed after Mike Shanahan was hired to coach the Broncos in 1995. He built a new team around Elway and young offensive stars Terrell Davis, Shannon Sharpe, and Rod Smith. The Denver defense mixed youth and experience, with Steve Atwater, Bill Romanowski, and Neil Smith leading the way.

In 1997, the Broncos put it all together and beat the Green Bay Packers in Super Bowl XXXII. They repeated as champions the

LEFT: John Elway scans the field for an open teammate.
ABOVE: Terrell Davis runs for a touchdown against the Philadelphia Eagles.

following year with a victory over the Atlanta Falcons in Super Bowl XXXIII. Even though Elway retired after the second championship, the team's winning *tradition* carried on.

From 1999 to 2006, the Broncos returned to the playoffs four times. The key to Denver's success was its rushing attack. It was so good during this time that six different runners gained more than 1,000 yards in a single season. The defense continued to be strong, thanks to stars such as Al Wilson, John Lynch, Champ Bailey, and Trevor Pryce. The Broncos made it back to the championship game of the **American Football Conference (AFC)** in 2005.

After that season, Denver went five years without making the playoffs. The Broncos started to rebuild their team around young stars such as Ryan Clady, Jay Cutler, Brandon Marshall, and Knowshon Moreno. But the team struggled to win. It was then that the Broncos turned to a familiar face.

ELVIS DUMERVIL

Denver hired Elway to run the team off the field. In 2011, after Tim Tebow became the starting quarterback, the Broncos went on an amazing winning streak. Tebow's statistics weren't very impressive, but he had a way of inspiring his teammates when the pressure was on. **Veteran** running back Willis McGahee gained more than 1,000 yards. The Denver defense—led by Bailey, Von Miller, and Elvis Dumervil—did a great job all season. At the end of the year, the Broncos were **AFC West** champions!

After the season, the Broncos faced a tough decision. Despite Tebow's great performance, they had a chance to bring Peyton Manning to Denver. Manning was an **All-Pro** passer who had won the Super Bowl with the Indianapolis Colts. The Broncos chose to go with Manning and traded Tebow. As the 2012 season began, football fans in Denver were thinking Super Bowl for the first time since the glory days of Elway.

LEFT: Al Wilson
ABOVE: Elvis Dumervil

Home Turf

The Broncos have a big home-field advantage. Denver is a mile above *sea level*, which makes the air thinner and harder to breathe. In fact, the team's stadium has been known for years as "Mile High." Because the Broncos live and train in this environment, they often have more energy at the end of a tough game.

Denver's first Mile High Stadium was built in 1960. In 2001, the team opened a new stadium next to the site of the old one. As in the old stadium, the seats are very close to the playing field, which means players can hear everything the fans say. Outside the stadium, there is a large model horse named Bucky Bronco. He used to sit atop the scoreboard in the team's original stadium.

BY THE NUMBERS

- The Broncos' stadium has 76,125 seats.
- The stadium cost $364.9 million to build.
- As of 2012, the Broncos had welcomed 22 players into their Ring of Fame, which forms a circle along the stadium's upper deck.

Fans stand and cheer as they await the kickoff of a Broncos game.

Dressed for Success

Denver's first colors were brown and yellow. The Broncos selected them after finding uniforms left over from a college all-star game. In 1962, Denver switched to orange, white, and blue. The team still uses these colors today, although the blue is much darker.

Denver's uniform has changed quite a bit over the years. For many seasons, orange was the primary color. That's how the Orange Crush defense of the 1970s got its nickname. In 1997, the team introduced new uniforms with blue as the main color.

The team *logo* has always shown a bronco, or wild horse. In 1968, Denver *unveiled* a logo that featured a bronco kicking its way through a big *D*. It became one of the NFL's most famous logos. In the 1990s, the team updated it with a design that looked more modern.

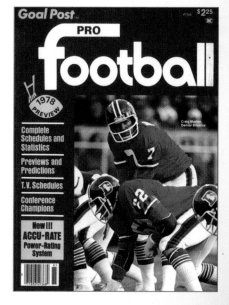

LEFT: Champ Bailey wears the Broncos' dark blue home uniform.
ABOVE: This magazine shows Craig Morton in the orange uniform from the 1970s.

15

We Won!

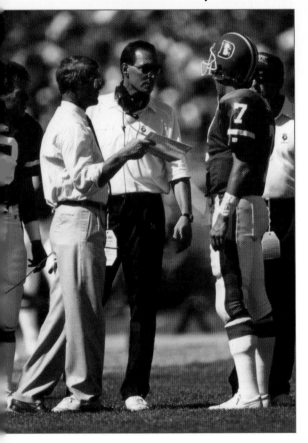

I t takes a while to build a championship football team. The Broncos waited 14 seasons before they had their first winning record. Soon after that, they rose to the top of the AFC. In 1977, the Broncos became conference champs. Although they lost to the Dallas Cowboys in Super Bowl XII, "Broncomania" was born.

Denver continued to field good teams. The Broncos won the AFC championship again in 1986, 1987, and 1989 under coach Dan Reeves. Their leader on the field was John Elway, who produced one amazing playoff victory after another. Elway never believed his team was out of a game. He was at his best in the final minutes when the pressure was at its most intense. Unfortunately, the first three times he brought the Broncos

to the Super Bowl, they lost badly. As Elway neared the end of his career, Denver fans feared they had missed their chance to win it all.

In 1995, Mike Shanahan was named head coach. He surrounded Elway with talented players who were hungry for a championship. With a strong supporting cast helping out, Elway became an even better quarterback. In 1997, the Broncos won their fifth AFC championship. Elway benefitted from a great rushing attack. Terrell Davis gained 1,750 yards and scored 15 touchdowns. Nine times that season, Denver topped 30 points in a game.

LEFT: John Elway talks to Dan Reeves and his staff on the sidelines.
ABOVE: Terrell Davis breaks a tackle in Super Bowl XXXII.

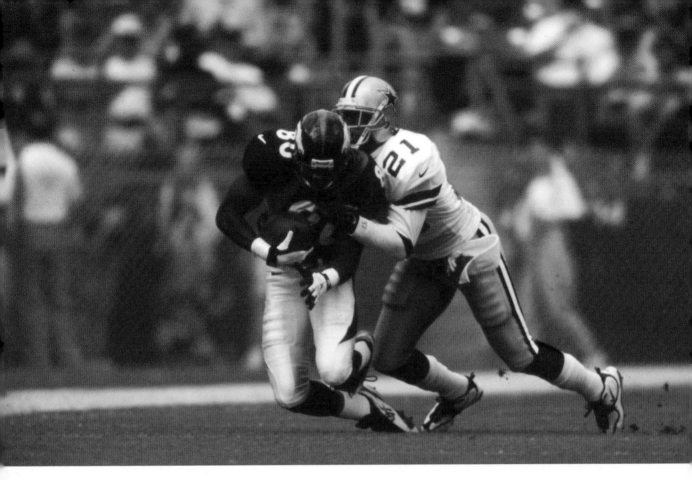

That January, the Broncos faced Brett Favre and the Green Bay Packers in Super Bowl XXXII. Davis was unstoppable. He shredded the Green Bay defense for 157 yards and three touchdowns. The third came late in the fourth quarter to give the Broncos a 31–24 lead. Favre drove his team into Denver territory, but the Broncos batted down two desperate passes for the victory. More than one million fans attended a parade for the champions in Denver two days later.

The victory over the Packers was just the beginning for the Broncos. They stayed on a roll the following season and set a team record by winning 14 games during the regular season. Elway and Davis had great years again. Receivers Shannon Sharpe, Rod Smith, and Ed McCaffrey were just as dangerous. Together they caught more than 200 passes and scored 26 touchdowns.

The Broncos faced the Atlanta Falcons in Super Bowl XXXIII. This time, the field opened up

for Elway as the Falcons focused on stopping Davis. The veteran quarterback passed for 336 yards and a touchdown. He also ran for a score. Meanwhile, the Denver defense did not allow a touchdown until the closing minutes of the game. By then it was too late for Atlanta. The Broncos won easily, 34–19. Denver had repeated as Super Bowl champs. In his final appearance as a Bronco, Elway was named the game's **Most Valuable Player (MVP)**.

LEFT: Rod Smith makes a catch against Deion Sanders, one of the NFL's best pass defenders.   **ABOVE**: John Elway hugs the football after scoring a touchdown against the Atlanta Falcons.

Go-To Guys

To be a true star in the NFL, you need more than fast feet and a big body. You have to be a "go-to guy"—someone the coach wants on the field at the end of a big game. Broncos fans have had a lot to cheer about over the years, including these great stars …

THE PIONEERS

LIONEL TAYLOR
END
DENVER BRONCOS

LIONEL TAYLOR   Receiver

• BORN: 8/15/1935   • PLAYED FOR TEAM: 1960 TO 1966

In his first season in pro football, Lionel Taylor rode the bench for the Chicago Bears. The Broncos signed him the following year, and he became a star. Taylor led the AFL in receiving in five of the league's first six seasons.

RICH JACKSON   Defensive Lineman

• BORN: 7/22/1941   • PLAYED FOR TEAM: 1967 TO 1972

Rich Jackson was very difficult to block. He was nicknamed "Tombstone" because he liked to bury opposing quarterbacks. Jackson was the first Bronco to be voted an NFL All-Pro.

FLOYD LITTLE   Running Back

- Born: 7/4/1942   • Played for Team: 1967 to 1975

From 1968 to 1973, Floyd Little was Denver's best all-around player. Fans called him "The **Franchise**" because he was the most important player on the team. He was voted into the **Hall of Fame** in 2010.

RILEY ODOMS   Tight End

- Born: 3/1/1950
- Played for Team: 1972 to 1983

During the 1970s, no Bronco was tougher than Riley Odoms. The rules of the day allowed the defense to be very rough with pass receivers. But no one could keep Odoms from making big plays.

TOM JACKSON   Linebacker

- Born: 4/4/1951   • Played for Team: 1973 to 1986

Tom Jackson was the heart and soul of Denver's Orange Crush defense. What he lacked in speed and size, he made up for with his desire to win. Jackson **intercepted** 20 passes during his career and returned three for touchdowns.

RANDY GRADISHAR   Linebacker

- Born: 3/3/1952   • Played for Team: 1974 to 1983

Randy Gradishar looked like he was born to play linebacker. He was big and fast—and *durable*. Gradishar never missed a game during his career.

LEFT: Lionel Taylor
ABOVE: Riley Odoms

JOHN ELWAY   Quarterback

• BORN: 6/28/1960   • PLAYED FOR TEAM: 1983 TO 1998

John Elway was one of the most talented quarterbacks ever. He ran with

the ball like a halfback and could throw touchdown passes from anywhere on the field. Elway was at his best late in games. No one was cooler under pressure.

KARL MECKLENBURG   Linebacker

• BORN: 9/1/1960   • PLAYED FOR TEAM: 1983 TO 1994

More than 350 players were taken in the 1983 draft before Karl Mecklenburg. He took that as a challenge to prove himself. In 12 seasons with the Broncos, Mecklenburg was voted All-Pro three times.

SHANNON SHARPE   Tight End

• BORN: 6/26/1968   • PLAYED FOR TEAM: 1990 TO 1999 & 2002 TO 2003

Shannon Sharpe was one of the most talkative players in the NFL. He backed up his words by becoming one of the most dangerous receivers ever to play tight end.

TERRELL DAVIS   Running Back

• BORN: 10/28/1972   • PLAYED FOR TEAM: 1995 TO 2001

Terrell Davis was fast and powerful. It often took two or three defenders to tackle him. His best season came in 1998 when he rushed for 2,008 yards and 21 touchdowns. Despite painful injuries, he retired as the team's all-time leading rusher.

ROD SMITH   Wide Receiver

- BORN: 5/15/1970   - PLAYED FOR TEAM: 1995 TO 2006

Rod Smith caught just 22 passes in his first two seasons in Denver. Once the Broncos made him a starter, he became their best receiver. In 2001, Smith led the NFL with 113 receptions and scored 12 touchdowns.

CHAMP BAILEY   Defensive Back

- BORN: 6/22/1978   - FIRST YEAR WITH TEAM: 2004

The Broncos traded for Champ Bailey after four seasons as a star with the Washington Redskins. He was even better as a Bronco. Bailey was named All-Pro in each of his first three seasons in Denver. In 2006, he led the NFL with 10 interceptions.

PEYTON MANNING   Quarterback

- BORN: 3/24/1976   - FIRST YEAR WITH TEAM: 2012

Many teams wanted to sign Peyton Manning to be their quarterback in 2012. In the end, the Broncos were the team that Manning wanted to lead. After breaking many NFL passing records with the Indianapolis Colts, he set his sights on leading Denver back to the Super Bowl.

LEFT: Karl Mecklenburg
RIGHT: Peyton Manning

Calling the Shots

The Broncos have always looked for coaches who can make their players believe that they can win any game. John Ralston fit that mold. When he arrived in Denver in 1972, the team had never had a winning season. One year later, the Broncos were competing for first place in the AFC West. Ralston's success was due in large part to his great defenses.

In 1977, Denver made Red Miller its coach. He had been one of Ralston's assistants, so he knew the players very well. Miller finished the job Ralston had started. In his first season, the Broncos made it all the way to the Super Bowl.

During the 1980s, Dan Reeves took the Broncos back to the Super Bowl three times. During his NFL career, Reeves had played for Tom Landry, one of the greatest coaches in football history. Reeves learned that winning took a team effort, not just a few superstars. Getting the Broncos to understand this wasn't easy, especially because their quarterback was

LEFT: Red Miller
RIGHT: Mike Shanahan

John Elway. Once they learned that lesson, they were nearly unstoppable.

Denver's greatest coach was Mike Shanahan. He was always prepared. Each week, Shanahan built a game plan that made the most of Elway's strengths and took advantage of the weak spots on other teams. But it was a great running attack that turned out to be the key to success for Denver. The Broncos won the Super Bowl in Shanahan's second and third seasons.

After Elway retired, Shanahan's system still worked wonders. From 1998 to 2006, the Broncos used six different running backs—Terrell Davis, Olandis Gary, Mike Anderson, Clinton Portis, Rueben Droughns, and Tatum Bell. Each player ran for more than 1,000 yards! John Fox also favored a strong rushing attack. He became Denver's coach in 2011 and led the team back to the playoffs.

One Great Day

When the Broncos traded for John Elway after the 1983 draft, they knew they would have to wait for him to become a winning quarterback. During Elway's first three years, he threw more interceptions than touchdowns and failed to win a playoff game. The fans were starting to lose their patience.

In 1986, Elway finally had the season everyone had been expecting. He threw for 3,485 yards and 19 touchdowns. The Broncos finished first in the AFC West, and then beat the New England Patriots in the playoffs. That set up a showdown with the Cleveland Browns in the **AFC Championship Game**.

Playing in Cleveland on a cold January day, the Broncos led by a **field goal** in the fourth quarter. With the home crowd behind them, the Browns stormed back to score 10 points and take a 20–13 lead. Elway had time enough for one last drive. Starting on his own 2-yard line, he led the Broncos down the field on an amazing touchdown march that sent the game into **overtime**.

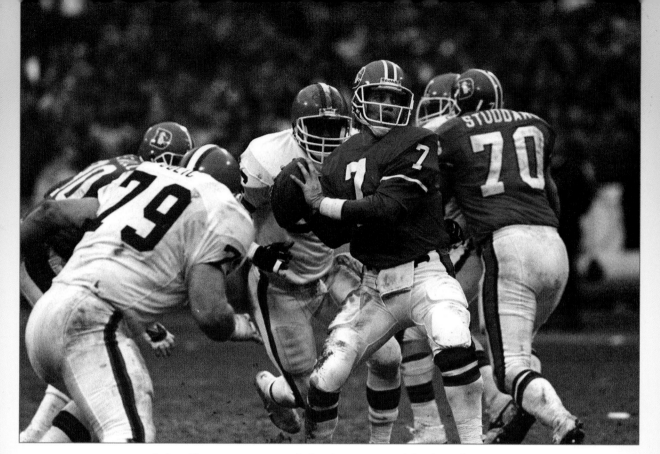

John Elway waits until the last second before firing
a pass against the Browns.

In the extra period, the Denver defense forced the Browns to punt. With the ball back in his hands, Elway completed two long passes to move the Broncos deep into Cleveland territory. Coach Dan Reeves then signaled for kicker Rich Karlis, who booted the winning field goal. The Broncos celebrated their first AFC championship!

Denver would win four more conference titles with Elway at quarterback. He would perform many more remarkable feats. To this day, however, his 98-yard masterpiece against the Browns is still known as "The Drive."

Legend Has It

Did the Broncos "un-retire" a number in 2012?

ABOVE: Frank Tripucka

LEGEND HAS IT that they did. The Broncos are one of many sports teams that retire numbers of important players in team history. In 1963, they honored Frank Tripucka, who wore #18. Tripucka was Denver's first star and the first quarterback to throw for more than 3,000 yards. When Peyton Manning joined the Broncos in 2012, Tripucka said he would be happy to let the team's new quarterback wear his old number. Manning gladly took it. "It's been retired for 50 years," Tripucka joked. "That's long enough!"

Did the Broncos once need snowmobiles to make it to a game?

LEGEND HAS IT that they did. In 1997, a blizzard hit Denver the same day the team was supposed to fly to Buffalo for a game against the Bills. Many players were stranded on their way to the airport. Broncos fans organized a snowmobile "rescue mission." The next day, the team plane took off with everyone on board.

Who wore the ugliest socks in football?

LEGEND HAS IT that the Broncos did. Football socks are usually either one solid color, or a mix of horizontal stripes. In the early 1960s, the Broncos wore socks with brown vertical stripes. Despite complaints from players and fans, the team didn't change its socks until 1962. When the new socks arrived, the players made a pile of the old ones and set it on fire.

It Really Happened

The 2011 season will forever be remembered as the "Year of Tim Tebow" in Denver. After the Broncos lost four of their first five games, coach John Fox made Tebow his starting quarterback. No one was sure what to expect. Tebow had been a great college star, but few thought he would continue his success in the NFL. Most experts said his arm was not strong enough. They thought he would be better as a running back or a tight end.

Tebow never doubted his own ability. In his first game, Denver trailed the Miami Dolphins 15–0 with three minutes to go in the fourth quarter. No team in NFL history had ever come back to win in this situation. That didn't bother Tebow. He led the Broncos to an 18–15 victory in overtime!

After a loss the following week, Tebow led the Broncos to six wins in a row—including two more thrilling overtime victories. The Denver defense kept the score close, and then Tebow would make a game-winning play. The Broncos believed they could beat anyone ... and Tebow made believers out of millions of NFL fans. He

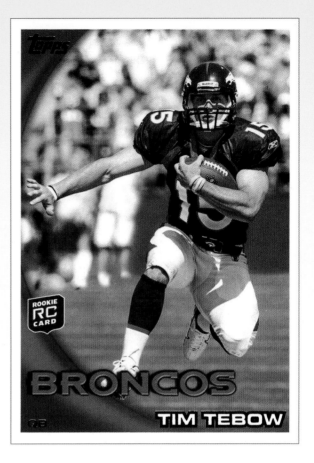

This trading card of Tim Tebow shows him doing what most experts said he did best.

finished the regular season with 12 touchdowns through the air and six more on the ground. His record as a starter was 7–4.

Against all odds, the Broncos won the AFC West and reached the playoffs for the first time since 2005. They hosted the Pittsburgh Steelers in the first round of the **postseason**. Incredibly, Denver played its fourth overtime game of the season.

The Broncos led late in the fourth quarter, but Pittsburgh tied the game. On Denver's first offensive play of the extra period, Tebow fired a pass to Demaryius Thomas, who caught the ball and raced 80 yards for the winning score. The quarterback who was criticized for his weak throwing arm had just thrown the longest overtime scoring pass in NFL history.

Team Spirit

Denver fans go completely wild for the Broncos. In fact, few teams in professional football have fans who are as *passionate*. More than one million fans lined the streets of Denver for the parades celebrating the team's Super Bowl victories during the 1990s.

Getting a ticket for a Broncos game is almost impossible. The team's new stadium has been *sold out* ever since it opened in 2001. Inside the stadium, the fans are so loud that opposing players have to scream to talk to each other. When an opposing quarterback misses a receiver with a pass, the fans chant, "In-com-plete!" The crowd noise in Denver is known as "Rocky Mountain Thunder."

"Thunder" also happens to be the name of the team **mascot**. Thunder is an Arabian stallion that looks like the logo on the Denver helmet. Every time the Broncos score a touchdown, he charges onto the field.

LEFT: Even in the rain, there is no place Denver fans would rather be than in Mile High Stadium.   **ABOVE**: This pin was sold at the "old" Mile High in the early 1960s.

Timeline

In this timeline, each Super Bowl is listed under the year it was played. Remember that the Super Bowl is held early in the year and is actually part of the previous season. For example, Super Bowl XLVI was played on February 5, 2012, but it was the championship of the 2011 NFL season.

1962
Gene Mingo leads the AFL in field goals for the second time.

1983
John Elway joins the team.

1960
The Broncos play their first season.

1973
Coach John Ralston leads the Broncos to their first winning season.

1978
The Broncos reach the Super Bowl for the first time.

Eldon Danenhauer was one of the team's top players in 1960.

Rick Upchurch was an All-Pro in 1978.

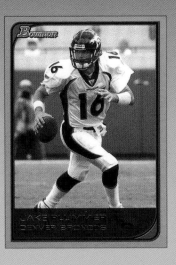

Jake
Plummer

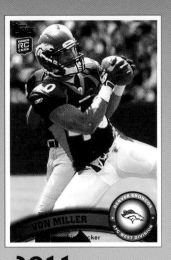

Von
Miller

1998
The Broncos win their
first Super Bowl.

2006
Jake Plummer leads the
team to a 13–3 record.

2011
Von Miller is named
to the Pro Bowl as a
rookie.

1990
The Broncos reach the
Super Bowl for the third
time in four seasons.

1999
The Broncos repeat as
Super Bowl champs.

2009
Elvis Dumervil leads
the NFL with 17 **sacks**.

Shannon
Sharpe caught
seven passes
in Denver's two
Super Bowl
victories.

Fun Facts

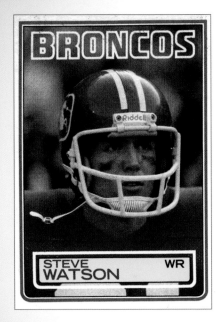

LOOKING SHARP

During the 1980s, Steve Watson had one of the NFL's coolest nicknames: The Blade. Watson sliced through defenses to lead the league with 13 touchdown catches in 1981. He also had a 95-yard scoring play—the longest of the year.

NAME GAME

John Elway led the Broncos to so many comeback victories that opponents actually had a name for losing to him: "Getting Elwayed."

FAMILY AFFAIR

One of the players who helped the Broncos become a winning team in the 1970s was middle linebacker Tom Graham. After his playing days, he ran a company that made air fresheners in the shape of football helmets. Graham's son Daniel followed in his footsteps and played for the Broncos from 2007 to 2010.

ABOVE: Steve Watson   **RIGHT**: Gene Mingo

MINGO MANIA

Gene Mingo did a little bit of everything for the Broncos in the 1960s—running the ball, catching passes, and returning kicks. Mingo's greatest skill was as a kicker. He led the AFL in field goals and points twice. Mingo was the first African American to be a full-time kicker.

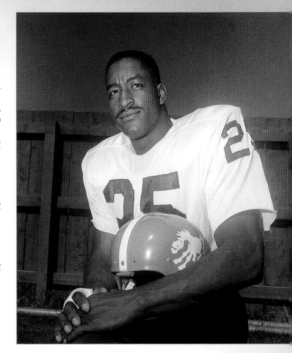

FLYING HIGH

Austin William "Goose" Gonsoulin set a team record with 11 interceptions in Denver's first season in 1960. Champ Bailey came within one of tying that mark in 2006.

GOOD FRIENDS, GREAT HANDS

Mark Jackson, Vance Johnson, and Ricky Nattiel were best buddies and star receivers for the Broncos in the 1980s. They were nicknamed the "Three Amigos" after the 1986 movie starring Steve Martin.

MISSION COMPLETE

Tim Tebow had his best passing game as a Bronco in his first playoff game. He completed 10 passes for 316 yards. His average of 31.6 yards per completion set an NFL postseason record.

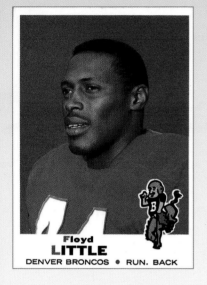

Floyd
LITTLE
DENVER BRONCOS • RUN. BACK

"I waited over thirty years for this day to come. Now I sit here living my dream, and this truly is a dream."

▶ **Floyd Little,** *on being voted into the Hall of Fame*

"He created the opportunity for me and others to come to Denver and play for a great franchise with the best fans in the world."

▶ **Ed McCaffrey,** *on how Floyd Little made the Broncos Denver's most popular team*

"If you're not improving, chances are you're not going to win."

▶ **Mike Shanahan,** *on why even the best teams always look to get better*

"We didn't know how far we were going. We didn't have a clue. The Broncos had never even been in the playoffs, so how could anyone expect us to go to the Super Bowl?"

▶ **Craig Morton,** *on the 1977 Broncos*

"I've experienced the highest of highs and lowest of lows. You learn a lot more from the lows because it makes you pay attention to what you're doing."

▶ **John Elway,** *on the lessons a player can learn from defeat*

"He is a rare talent, there is no doubt. He has the things that you cannot coach."

▶ **John Fox,** *on Von Miller*

"It's the best feeling in football. I'd rather have that over a touchdown … over anything."

▶ **Elvis Dumervil,** *on what it's like to make the quarterback fumble*

"We're going to do whatever we can to win right now."

▶ **Peyton Manning,** *on joining the Broncos in 2012*

LEFT: Floyd Little
ABOVE: John Elway

Great Debates

People who root for the Broncos love to compare their favorite moments, teams, and players. Some debates have been going on for years! How would you settle these classic football arguments?

Terrell Davis was the greatest running back in Denver history ....

... because he owns almost every team record. Davis (   ) ran for more than 7,500 yards as a Bronco, including 2,008 yards in 1998! That season, he led Denver to the Super Bowl and was named the league MVP. Davis also lived up to his nickname, "TD." In 1998, he broke his own team record by running for 21 touchdowns.

No one was greater than Floyd Little ....

... because for most of his career, he was the only hope the Broncos had of winning. Little had true star power. Even when everyone in the stadium—including the other team—knew he would get the ball, the defense could not slow him down. From 1968 to 1973, there were many great runners in pro football. None of them gained more yards during that time than Little.

The Orange Crush defense was the best in team history ....

... because for one season, in 1977, it was practically perfect. Lyle Alzado, Barney Chavous, and Rubin Carter formed a fearsome three-man front line. Behind them were four great linebackers: Tom Jackson, Randy Gradishar, Joe Rizzo, and Bob Swenson. No team could run the ball against Denver that season. In the playoffs, the Broncos beat two dangerous offensive teams—the Pittsburgh Steelers and Oakland Raiders—to reach the Super Bowl.

The Denver defense of the 1990s was even better ....

... because it helped the team win the Super Bowl two years in a row. The Denver defense did not have a fun nickname, but it made big plays all the time. Its stars included Steve Atwater (RIGHT), Neil Smith, and Bill Romanowski. Atwater was a perfect example of how dangerous the Broncos were. In 1997, he intercepted two passes, recovered two fumbles, had a sack, and scored a touchdown.

For the Record

The great Broncos teams and players have left their marks on the record books. These are the "best of the best" ...

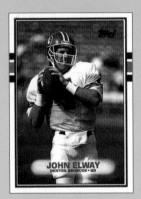

John Elway

Dan Reeves

BRONCOS AWARD WINNERS

WINNER	AWARD	YEAR
Billy Joe	AFL Rookie of the Year	1963
Willie Brown	AFL All-Star Game MVP	1964
Craig Morton	Comeback Player of the Year	1977
Red Miller	NFL Coach of the Year	1977
Randy Gradishar	NFL Defensive Player of the Year	1978
Terrell Davis	NFL Offensive Player of the Year	1996
Terrell Davis	Super Bowl XXXII MVP	1998
Terrell Davis	NFL Offensive Player of the Year	1998
John Elway	Super Bowl XXXIII MVP	1999
Mike Anderson	NFL Offensive Rookie of the Year	2000
Clinton Portis	NFL Offensive Rookie of the Year	2002
Von Miller	NFL Defensive Rookie of the Year	2011

This pennant celebrates Denver's trip to the Super Bowl in 1987.

BRONCOS ACHIEVEMENTS

ACHIEVEMENT	YEAR
AFC West Champions	1977
AFC Champions	1977
AFC West Champions	1978
AFC West Champions	1984
AFC West Champions	1986
AFC Champions	1986
AFC West Champions	1987
AFC Champions	1987
AFC West Champions	1989
AFC Champions	1989
AFC West Champions	1991
AFC West Champions	1996
AFC Champions	1997
Super Bowl XXXII Champions	1997*
AFC Champions	1998
Super Bowl XXXIII Champions	1998*
AFC West Champions	2005
AFC West Champions	2011

Super Bowls are played early the following year, but the game is counted as the championship of this season.

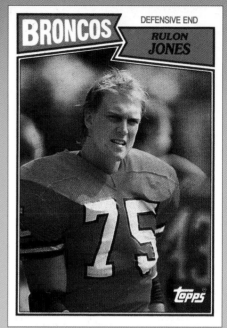

BRONCOS — DEFENSIVE END — RULON JONES

ABOVE: Rulon Jones was a leader of the defense for the 1986 and 1987 champs.
BELOW: Jim Turner and Lyle Alzado were stars of the 1977 AFC champions.

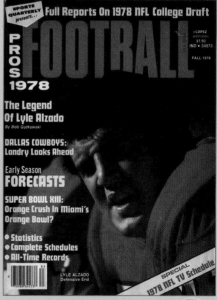

Full Reports On 1978 NFL College Draft

PROS FOOTBALL 1978

The Legend Of Lyle Alzado
By Bob Gutkowski

DALLAS COWBOYS: Landry Looks Ahead

Early Season FORECASTS

SUPER BOWL XIII: Orange Crush In Miami's Orange Bowl?

• Statistics
• Complete Schedules
• All-Time Records

LYLE ALZADO Defensive End

SPECIAL 1978 NFL TV Schedule

Pinpoints

The history of a football team is made up of many smaller stories. These stories take place all over the map—not just in the city a team calls "home." Match the pushpins on these maps to the **Team Facts**, and you will begin to see the story of the Broncos unfold!

TEAM FACTS

1. Denver, Colorado—*The Broncos play their home games here.*
2. San Diego, California—*The Broncos won Super Bowl XXXII here.*
3. Port Angeles, Washington—*John Elway was born here.*
4. Dallas, Texas—*Von Miller was born here.*
5. New Orleans, Louisiana—*The Broncos played in their first Super Bowl here.*
6. Montrose, Georgia—*Demaryius Thomas was born here.*
7. Miami, Florida—*The Broncos won Super Bowl XXXIII here.*
8. Warren, Ohio—*Randy Gradishar was born here.*
9. Chicago, Illinois—*Otis Armstrong was born here.*
10. New Haven, Connecticut—*Floyd Little was born here.*
11. London, England—*The Broncos played in the 1987 American Bowl* here.*
12. Makati City, Philippines—*Tim Tebow was born here.*

* The American Bowl was the annual NFL game played outside the United States.

Otis Armstrong

Glossary

AFC CHAMPIONSHIP GAME—The game played to determine which AFC team will go to the Super Bowl.

AFC WEST—A division for teams that play in the western part of the country.

ALL-PRO—An honor given to the best players at their positions at the end of each season.

AMERICAN FOOTBALL CONFERENCE (AFC)—One of two groups of teams that make up the NFL.

AMERICAN FOOTBALL LEAGUE (AFL)—The football league that began play in 1960 and later merged with the NFL.

CONSISTENT—Doing something again and again at the same level of performance.

DECADES—Periods of 10 years; also specific periods, such as the 1950s.

DRAFTED—Chosen from a group of the best college players. The NFL draft is held each spring.

DURABLE—Able to avoid or withstand injury.

FIELD GOAL—A goal from the field, kicked over the crossbar and between the goal posts. A field goal is worth three points.

FRANCHISE—Another term for a sports team.

HALL OF FAME—The museum in Canton, Ohio, where football's greatest players are honored. A player voted into the Hall of Fame is sometimes called a "Hall of Famer."

INTERCEPTED—Caught in the air by a defensive player.

LOGO—A symbol or design that represents a company or team.

MASCOT—An animal or person believed to bring a group good luck.

MOST VALUABLE PLAYER (MVP)—The award given each year to the league's best player; also given to the best player in the Super Bowl and Pro Bowl.

NATIONAL FOOTBALL LEAGUE (NFL)—The league that started in 1920 and is still operating today.

OVERTIME—The extra period played when a game is tied after 60 minutes.

PASSIONATE—Intensely emotional.

PLAYOFFS—The games played after the regular season to determine which teams play in the Super Bowl.

POSTSEASON—Another term for playoffs.

PROFESSIONAL—Paid to play.

ROOKIE—A player in his first year.

SACKS—Tackles of the quarterback behind the line of scrimmage.

SEA LEVEL—The low point used when measuring the height of geographical features, such as mountains.

SKYROCKETED—Rose quickly and by large numbers.

SOLD OUT—All tickets sold.

SUPER BOWL—The championship of the NFL, played between the winners of the National Football Conference and American Football Conference.

TRADITION—A belief or custom that is handed down from generation to generation.

UNVEILED—Made public.

VETERAN—Having great experience.

OVERTIME

TEAM SPIRIT introduces a great way to stay up to date with your team! Visit our **OVERTIME** link and get connected to the latest and greatest updates. **OVERTIME** serves as a young reader's ticket to an exclusive web page—with more stories, fun facts, team records, and photos of the Broncos. Content is updated during and after each season. The **OVERTIME** feature also enables readers to send comments and letters to the author! Log onto:

www.norwoodhousepress.com/library.aspx
and click on the tab: **TEAM SPIRIT** to access **OVERTIME**.

Read all the books in the series to learn more about professional sports. For a complete listing of the baseball, basketball, football, and hockey teams in the **TEAM SPIRIT** series, visit our website at:

www.norwoodhousepress.com/library.aspx

On the Road

THE DENVER BRONCOS
1701 Bryant Street
Denver, Colorado 80204
303-649-9000
www.denverbroncos.com

THE PRO FOOTBALL HALL OF FAME
2121 George Halas Drive NW
Canton, Ohio 44708
330-456-8207
www.profootballhof.com

On the Bookshelf

To learn more about the sport of football, look for these books at your library or bookstore:

Frederick, Shane. *The Best of Everything Football Book.* North Mankato, Minnesota: Capstone Press, 2011.

Jacobs, Greg. *The Everything Kids' Football Book: The All-Time Greats, Legendary Teams, Today's Superstars—And Tips on Playing Like a Pro.* Avon, Massachusetts: Adams Media Corporation, 2010.

Editors of *Sports Illustrated for Kids. 1st and 10: Top 10 Lists of Everything in Football.* New York, New York: Sports Illustrated Books, 2011.

Index

PAGE NUMBERS IN **BOLD** REFER TO ILLUSTRATIONS.

Alzado, Lyle 7, 41, **43**
Anderson, Mike 25, 42
Armstrong, Otis 7, 45, **45**
Atwater, Steve 9, 41, **41**
Bailey, Champ 10, 11, **14**, 23, 37
Bell, Tatum 25
Brown, Willie 42
Carter, Rubin 41
Chavous, Barney 41
Clady, Ryan 11
Danenhauer, Eldon 6, **34**
Davis, Terrell 9, **9**, 17, **17**, 18, 19, 22, 25, 40, **40**, 42
Denson, Al 6
Droughns, Rueben 25
Dumervil, Elvis 11, **11**, 35, 39
Elway, John **8**, 9, 10, 11, 16, **16**, 17, 19, **19**, 22, 25, 26, 27, **27**, 34, 36, 39, **39**, 42, **42**, 45
Favre, Brett 18
Fox, John 25, 30, 39
Gary, Olandis 25
Gonsoulin, Goose 37
Gradishar, Randy 7, **7**, 21, 41, 42, 45
Graham, Daniel 36
Graham, Tom 36
Jackson, Mark 37
Jackson, Rich 6, 20
Jackson, Tom 7, 21, 41
Joe, Billy 42
Johnson, Vance 37
Jones, Rulon **43**
Karlis, Rich 27
Landry, Tom 24
Little, Floyd 6, **6**, 21, 38, **38**, 40, 45
Lynch, John 10
Manning, Peyton 11, 23, **23**, 28, 39

Marshall, Brandon 11
Martin, Steve 37
McBean, Ryan **4**
McCaffrey, Ed 19, 38
McFadin, Bud 6
McGahee, Willis 11
Mecklenburg, Karl 22, **22**
Miller, Red 7, 24, **24**, 42
Miller, Von **4**, 11, 35, **35**, 39, 42, 45
Mingo, Gene 6, 34, 37, **37**
Moreno, Knowshon 11
Morton, Craig 7, **15**, 38, 42
Moses, Haven 7
Nattiel, Ricky 37
Odoms, Riley 7, 21, **21**
Plummer, Jake 35, **35**
Portis, Clinton 25, 42
Pryce, Trevor 10
Ralston, John 7, 24, 34
Reeves, Dan 9, 16, **16**, 24, 27, 42, **42**
Rizzo, Joe 41
Romanowski, Bill 9, 41
Sanders, Deion **18**
Shanahan, Mike 9, 17, 25, **25**, 38
Sharpe, Shannon 9, 19, 22, **35**
Smith, Neil 9, 41
Smith, Rod 9, **18**, 19, 23
Swenson, Bob 41
Taylor, Lionel 6, 20, **20**
Tebow, Tim 11, 30, 31, **31**, 37, 45
Thomas, Demaryius 31, 45
Tripucka, Frank 6, 28, **28**
Turner, Jim **43**
Upchurch, Rick 7, **34**
Watson, Steve 36, **36**
Wilson, Al 10, **10**

About the Author

MARK STEWART has written more than 50 books on football and over 150 sports books for kids. He grew up in New York City during the 1960s rooting for the Giants and Jets, and was lucky enough to meet players from both teams. Mark comes from a family of writers. His grandfather was Sunday Editor of *The New York Times,* and his mother was Articles Editor of *Ladies' Home Journal* and *McCall's.* Mark has profiled hundreds of athletes over the past 25 years. He has also written several books about his native New York and New Jersey, his home today. Mark is a graduate of Duke University, with a degree in history. He lives and works in a home overlooking Sandy Hook, New Jersey. You can contact Mark through the Norwood House Press website.